COLLINS GEM
CATS
a mine of information

COLLINS GEM
ASTRO
牛鼠兔
a mine of information

COLLINS GEM

COLLINS GEM

COLLINS GEM

COLLINS GEM
HORSES
& PONIES
a mine of information

COLLINS GEM
INSECTS
a mine of information

COLLINS GEM
KINGS &
QUEENS
a mine of information

COLLINS GEM
MUSHROOMS
& TOADSTOOLS
a mine of information

COLLINS GEM
SNAKES
a mine of information

COLLINS GEM
SPIDERS
a mine of information

COLLINS GEM
STRESS
Survival Guide
a mine of information

COLLINS GEM
TAROT
a mine of information

COLLINS GEM
WINE
Guide
a mine of information

COLLINS GEM
WORLD
atlas
a mine of information

COLLINS GEM
YOGA
a mine of information

COLLINS GEM
ZODIAC
Types
a mine of information

COLLINS GEM

1950s

HarperCollins Publishers
PO Box, Glasgow G4 0NB

First published 1999

Reprint 10 9 8 7 6 5 4 3 2 1 0

ISBN 0 00 4723091-1 0

All pictures courtesy of Topham except: Popperfoto: pp. 12(t),
39(b), 41(r), 74(b), 96(t), 97(t), 115(l), 137(t), 176(b); M. Decet:
p. 29(b); Pictorial Press Ltd: pp. 38(r), 66(t), 82(b), 155(t);
P&O Ferries: p. 53(b); Allsport: p. 129(t); Mary Evans: pp. 59(t),
92(t); Christies: p. 149(t); Foundry Arts/D. P. Banfield: p. 87(b);
Foundry Arts: p. 100(r), 110(t), 147(b), 159(t), 162(t)
Associated Press: pp. 178(l); BFI Stills Posters and Designs: p. 40(b)

Created and produced by Flame Tree Publishing, part of
The Foundry Creative Media Co. Ltd
Crabtree Hall, Crabtree Lane, Fulham, London SW6 6TW

With special thanks to Josephine Cutts, Claire Dashwood,
Sue Evans, Helen Johnson, Dave Jones and Helen Tovey.

Printed in Italy by Amadeus S.p.A.

COLLINS GEM

1950s

**Nigel Gross Graeme Kay
Damian Wild Sue Wood**

HarperCollins*Publishers*

Contents

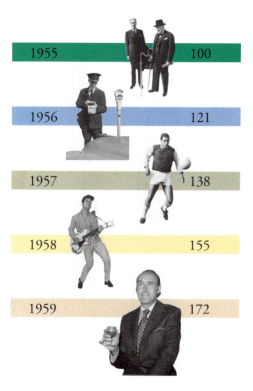

1955   100

1956   121

1957   138

1958   155

1959   172

How To Use This Book

This book covers a wide spectrum of the events that helped to define the 1950s. Events of world prominence – the first pacemaker, the Korean War, the Moon landings – and those of a less serious nature, such as the arrival of zebra crossings and the invention of the self-service supermarket. Sports, fashion, popular culture, science, the environment, literature, fine art, world news, cinema, theatre and music are all included.

1950s is divided in two ways: the contents page lists the page number at which each year of the decade begins, and every year is divided into individual months. Some months are contained on one page and some cover two pages. People, events and inventions all feature within each month, providing a comprehensive look at the spirit of the age. Every month also features a variety of entry lengths: some are simply a few words, some encompass several lines. In order to preserve the balance of the *Zeitgeist*, each theme is afforded prominence in rotation throughout the book; as a result, not every major entry refers necessarily to an event of international significance; it may refer to an important fashion trend, an exciting sporting moment or the death of a leading artist. Each month also includes boxed features, which contain events that happened in the year – but not necessarily in the month – in which they feature.

A comprehensive index at the end of the book assists readers who wish to look up specific entries or subjects but are unsure of the month or year in which they occurred.

A The page number appears in a colour-coded box that indicates which year you are looking at.

B Each month is indicated at the head of the initial page. Some months appear on one page, some over two depending on the number of relevant entries.

C The date of the event appears at the start of the entry. Entries with no date, but which are known to have happened in the specified month, appear at the top of the list.

D Entries differ in length from a few words to several lines.

E Every page is illustrated with topical photographs or drawings.

F Tint boxes indicate events that happened in the year, but not necessarily the month, in which they feature.

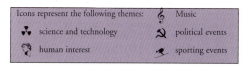

Icons represent the following themes:

- science and technology
- human interest
- Music
- political events
- sporting events

Introduction

After the bleakness of the Second World War, the 1950s saw a move towards a life without fear. Politically tempers still ran high, but the general public began to look forward to a bright future. The end of rationing, the start of the Space race and an incredible surge in technology heralded the beginning of a new and exciting, though sometimes bewildering, society. Stars like James Dean and Bill Haley brought about an overwhelming explosion of youth culture, the like of which had never been experienced before. The western world was changing – rapidly.

However, alongside this sparkling new world, there were still serious elements: the atomic age was a sudden, frightening reality; the Cold War was hotting up; Africa and Asia were experiencing

widespread unrest; a widely divided Europe was painfully easing its fragmented self back together; in the US a Communist witch-hunt was exploding and racial tensions were about to reach fever pitch. All this and the aftermath of the war.

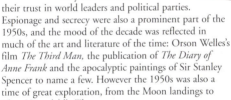

People had lost family and friends; they had also lost their trust in world leaders and political parties. Espionage and secrecy were also a prominent part of the 1950s, and the mood of the decade was reflected in much of the art and literature of the time: Orson Welles's film *The Third Man,* the publication of *The Diary of Anne Frank* and the apocalyptic paintings of Sir Stanley Spencer to name a few. However the 1950s was also a time of great exploration, from the Moon landings to Thor Heyerdahl's *The Kon-Tiki Expedition.* It was a decade of change and confusion but, most of all, of excitement.

1950

January 1950

6th Britain officially recognises Communist China.

 21st Author George Orwell dies of tuberculosis on the Scottish island of Jura. Orwell, whose real name was Eric Blair, was famed for his novels *Animal Farm* and *1984*, both written at the end of his life.

26th India goes one step further following its independence from British rule in August 1947. The country proclaims itself a sovereign democratic republic; a constitutional change that wins the full approval of Indian MPs.

Nizam of Hyderabad (right) takes oath to the New Republic

London is officially the world's largest city in terms of population – nearly 8.5 million people live there.

29th A trio of earthquakes claims 1,500 lives in Iran.

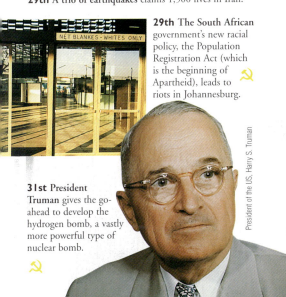

29th The South African government's new racial policy, the Population Registration Act (which is the beginning of Apartheid), leads to riots in Johannesburg.

NÉT BLANKES - WHITES ONLY

31st President **Truman** gives the go-ahead to develop the hydrogen bomb, a vastly more powerful type of nuclear bomb.

President of the US, Harry S. Truman

February 1950

Ingrid Bergman, photographed in 1964

2nd Ingrid Bergman gives birth to the illegitimate son of film director Roberto Rossellini in Rome. The couple later marry, but their marriage is annulled in 1960.

3rd A top nuclear scientist, Klaus Fuchs, is accused of spying. Seven years after being given a free rein at key UK and US research establishments, German-born Communist Dr Fuchs, 38, is charged with passing secrets to Soviet agents about how to build atomic bombs.

14th The USSR and China sign a Treaty of Friendship in Moscow.

The Charlie Brown Cartoon strip makes its first appearance in 1950.

18th The first Subscriber Trunk Dialling (STD) telephone connection commences between New York and New Jersey. For the first time calls can be made direct, without going through an operator.

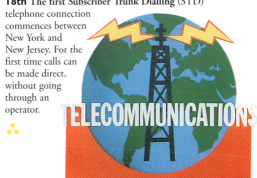

23rd The first-ever *Election Special* is transmitted on UK television. It sees a Labour win – albeit with a reduced majority.

28th The French government passes a law curbing the sale of Coca-Cola.

March 1950

1st In Taiwan, Chiang Kai-Shek re-forms the Chinese Nationalist Party under new policies.

3rd Alaska becomes the US's 49th 'star' as Washington votes to admit her to the United States.

8th It is revealed that the USSR has created an atomic bomb.

12th A flight carrying rugby fans crashes near Cardiff, causing 80 deaths. It is the world's worst air disaster to date.

29th Jean-Pierre Melville's version of Cocteau's erotically charged novel *Les Enfants Terribles* premieres in Paris.

1950 sees the world's first
Formula One motor-racing championship.

29th **The first colour television** pictures not requiring elaborate filters are demonstrated in the US by RCA. Earlier systems required coloured screens to flip over rapidly to produce coloured pictures and were incapable of receiving existing black and white transmissions.

31st *The Kon-Tiki Expedition*, Thor Heyerdahl's account of his epic voyage across the Pacific on a raft made of balsa logs, is published.

Explorer and author Thor Heyerdahl

April 1950

4th The German composer Kurt Weill, working partner of playwright Bertolt Brecht, dies of a heart attack.

8th The Delhi Pact is signed by India and Pakistan – each side agrees to support the rights of its minority residents.

German composer Kurt Weill

8th Russian ballet dancer Vaslav Nijinsky dies. Trained at the Imperial Ballet School in St Petersburg, Nijinsky was considered the greatest ballet dancer of the 20th century. He kept his reputation despite being diagnosed as a paranoid schizophrenic in 1917, after being interned in Hungary during the early part of the First World War.

18th The world's first jet-airmail service commences between Toronto and New York.

20th A patient at a New York hospital 'dies' twice, but is revived by a surgeon massaging his heart; he makes a full recovery.

24th A new **kingdom** of Jordan is created, with the absorption of the West Bank territory of Arab Palestine.

29th Footballer Denis Compton plays his last game for Arsenal as they defeat Liverpool 2–0 in the FA Cup Final.

Ajlun in the new Kingdom of Jordan

May 1950

Sir Malcolm Sargeant succeeds Sir Adrian Boult as principal conductor of the BBC Symphony Orchestra. Sargeant, a former music teacher, helped found the London Philharmonic Orchestra; took over as chief conductor of the Hallé Orchestra in 1939; and from 1942–50 was head of the Liverpool Philharmonic Orchestra.

1st The People's Republic of China outlaws polygamy and infanticide.

20th Diners Club issues the first charge cards in New York.

26th The end of UK petrol rationing creates record bank holiday traffic queues, according to the AA.

Good Friday traffic, Gorse Hill, Kent

June 1950

20th Newspapers claim screen star Judy Garland attempted to cut her own throat.

24–29th The West Indies cricket team win their first Test Match in England.

25th Communist North Korea catches the world napping as it launches a surprise invasion on its southern neighbour with a full-frontal attack by land, sea and air. The assault is later utterly condemned by the United Nations.

28th England lose 1–0 to the US in the first round of the World Cup. Uruguay go on to win the competition.

Soldiers carry Korean refugees to safety

July 1950

10th **The British government** announces that soap rationing is to end.

10th Frank Sinatra barely escapes with his clothes as a frenzied crowd screams its way through his performance at the London Palladium, his first British concert.

14th **The X-rated certificate** for films is introduced in the UK by the BBFC (British Board of Film Categorisation). The new certificate restricts access to certain films, where the subject matter is violent or sexually explicit, to those aged 16 and over.

22nd Belgium's King Leopold III arrives home at last after spending six years as an exile. His return precipitates a Socialist demonstration in Brussels. The protesters throng the city's streets the day after his arrival.

British Board of Film Categorisation inspect film

Air strikes off the Korean coast

26th British troops are mobilised to join the US forces fighting in support of South Korea. They reach Korea in August.

29th The first scheduled flight of a gas-turbine-powered airliner takes place between London and Paris.

31st Supermarket J. Sainsbury's opens its first self-service store in Croydon, South London.

August 1950

Decca releases the first 33 ⅓ rpm LPs for home use in the UK: *Trial by Jury* and Muchinger's recording of Bach's *Brandenburg Concertos* are among the first.

5th American Florence Chadwick sets a new record time for swimming the English Channel. Her 22-mile marine marathon from Cap Gris Nez to Dover knocked 60 minutes off the benchmark set in 1926 by Gertrude Ederle.

15th Princess Elizabeth gives birth to her second child, a daughter, Anne.

27th The British athletics team wins eight gold medals at the European Games.

Proud mother shows off Princess Anne

September 1950

United Nations troops reach the border of North Korea.

10th André Cayatte's *Justice et Faite* wins the Golden Lion award at the Venice Film Festival.

15th The period of time for National Service (compulsory military service for men) in the UK is extended to two years.

26th 80 miners die in an underground blaze at Creswell colliery in Derbyshire.

27th US scientists announce the discovery of a new way to turn the power of the atom

The nuclear power station of the future

into electricity. As yet the method is not practical for commercial use (and later proves never to be) but promises great things for the future. Details are being kept top secret.

Workers isolate colliery fire with sandbags

October 1950

2nd Britons can now benefit from Legal Aid – legal help for those who cannot afford to pay the usual fees.

6th The world's longest pipeline yet is opened. The 1705-km (1066-miles) long pipe runs between the Persian Gulf and the Mediterranean port of Sidon. It contains 30,000 tons of steel and cost ¼ billion dollars to construct.

17th & **31st Two British aircraft crash** in a month, one at Heathrow and one in North London: 56 die.

23rd Entertainer Al Jolson dies. Jolson was a Russian-born American who starred in the first talking picture, *The Jazz Singer*, in 1927.

Mill Hill air crash, 17 October

November 1950

The world's first pre-recorded music tapes went on sale this month in New York. Recording Associates Inc. released eight titles in the new medium. The first, *Cocktail Time*, features 11 popular tunes.

1st President Truman escapes unhurt in a failed assassination attempt at the US leader's temporary Washington residence.

US President Harry S. Truman

George Bernard Shaw photographed in 1948

2nd George Bernard Shaw dies at the age of 94 at his home in Ayot St Lawrence, Hertfordshire. The controversial Irish author, playwright and founder member of the socialist Fabian Society, won the Nobel Prize for Literature in 1925.

27th China enters the Korean War in support of North Korea. UN troops are pushed back.

December 1950

1st **The number of drive-in** cinemas in the US doubles to 4,400 in one year.

10th **Radical philosopher**, Bertrand Russell, wins the Nobel Prize for Literature, after the publication of *Marriage and Morals*. Recently he was also awarded the Order of Merit.

Drive-in cinemas become the place to be seen.

16th **Former child film star, Shirley Temple**, 22, marries businessman Charles Black.

25th **Tibetan spiritual leader**, the Dalai Lama, reportedly flees his homeland following an invasion by Chinese troops. The reports later prove to be untrue.

The 17-year-old Dalai Lama of Tibet

25th The Stone of Scone is snatched, by Scottish nationalists, from underneath the Coronation Chair in Westminster Abbey. The 458-pound stone, on which Scottish kings were once crowned, was taken from Scotland by Edward I in 1296.

27th German painter Max Beckmann, one of the greatest expressionist artists, dies in the US.

BBC television begins broadcasting the popular children's programme *Watch With Mother*.

The Stone of Scone finally returns to Scotland in 1996

1951

January 1951

Avalanches in the Alps claim over 100 lives.

1st Radio favourites *The Archers* can now be heard nationwide.

10th Sinclair Lewis, the first American to win the Nobel Prize for Literature, dies at the age of 75.

26th UN forces fail to stop Communist forces taking Seoul, in South Korea, for the second time.

Sinclair
Lewis and
his wife,
Dorothy

Ysanne
Churchman and
Norman Painting
recording *The
Archers*

1951 sees Fender release
the world's first electric bass guitar.

28th **In a dramatic move**, the Shah of Iran decrees that large areas of his own land are to be sold to peasants for farming.

The Shah of Iran

30th **German motor-car manufacturer** Ferdinand Porsche, creator of the Volkswagen and the sports cars that bear his name, dies.

Ferdinand Porsche's 911 classic

31st **A specially adapted P51 Mustang**, originally a US Second World War fighter, sets a new transatlantic speed record. Charles Blair Junior, the pilot and owner, took just 7 hours and 48 minutes to complete the flight. Despite his achievement Blair was disappointed not to have broken the 7-hour barrier!

February 1951

2nd Radiation monitors in the eastern US have detected increases in radiation levels following recent nuclear-bomb tests in the Nevada desert. Although the levels are very low there is concern that radiation is able to travel so far: airborne dust particles are being blamed.

Personnel radiation levels carefully checked in Eniwetok

8th Cecil Day-Lewis is elected the new Professor of Poetry at Oxford University.

8th King George VI gets the first pay rise of his reign, a 10 per cent increase.

9th Swedish-born actress Greta Garbo becomes a US citizen. The star of *Anna Karenina* has now retired from films.

26th US presidents are to serve a maximum of two terms – eight years – under the 22nd Amendment constitutional change.

Cecil Day-Lewis, also known as author Nicholas Blake

28th The England cricket team, captained by F. R. Brown, wins the fifth and final test by two wickets in Melbourne. It is the English side's first victory over the Australians, in Australia, since 1936.

Greta Garbo

March 1951

7th Iranian premier **General Ali Razmara** falls to an assassin's bullet when a religious extremist shoots him dead.

The assassinated General Ali Razmara

11th **The Free Presbyterian Church** is founded in Northern Ireland by the Reverend Ian Paisley.

24th **The annual Varsity** boat race is abandoned after the Oxford boat sinks. When the event is re-staged two days later, the Cambridge team wins by 12 lengths.

29th Orson Welles's **spy thriller**, *The Third Man*, wins an Oscar for best black and white photography. The film is based on the classic novel by Graham Greene.

April 1951

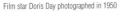

3rd Film star Doris Day marries producer Marty Melcher.

5th Convicted US spies Julius and Ethel Rosenberg are sentenced to death after being found guilty of passing stolen atomic secrets to the USSR. The Army Signal Corps electrical engineer, 32, and his wife, 35, protest their innocence to the end.

Film star Doris Day photographed in 1950

11th The Stone of Scone is found at Arbroath Abbey.

20th US air defences are put under the control of a computer nicknamed 'Whirlwind'. It is a great success.

29th The Austrian philosopher and author, Ludwig Wittgenstein, dies three days after his 62nd birthday.

The Rosenbergs, condemned to the electric chair

May 1951

Peter Walker wins the 24-hour Le Mans motor race. Walker, driving a Jaguar, becomes the first Briton to win the event since J. S. Hindmarsh in 1935. Walker, and co-driver Peter Whitehead, take the title with a winning speed of over 93.5 mph.

Festival of Britain cover girl

4th The Festival of Britain opens on London's South Bank. The Skylon, an aluminium tower, is the festival's symbol; the Royal Festival Hall is its centrepiece. The fireworks can be seen several miles away from the 27-acre main site, on which £8 million has been spent.

4th Tyrone Guthrie is appointed manager of London's Old Vic Theatre. The Anglo-Irish director, who was responsible for the invention of 'thrust stage

theatre', has worked in the US, Canada and the UK, and includes Laurence Olivier and Donald Wolfit among his distinguished collaborators.

UK pensionable age is decided

9th **The UK government decides to pay** state pensions at 60 for women and 65 for men.

12th **The US detonates** its first experimental H-bomb in the South Pacific. The tiny island of Eniwetok was rocked by a blast hundreds of times more powerful than the atomic bombs dropped on Japan during the Second World War.

16th **The John Lewis Partnership**, which runs several department stores, appoints a female Managing Director.

June 1951

4th American actor Tony Curtis weds actress Janet Leigh.

7th Missing British diplomats Guy Burgess and Donald MacLean are suspected of spying for the Soviets.

14th UNIVAC, an all-electronic computer that uses magnetic tape to store programs, goes on-line in the US.

18th The British government agrees to a proposed base for the US Air Force in Berkshire. The site of the air base is to be at Greenham Common, near Newbury. Local residents are not happy about the plans.

Anti-nuclear protests continued into the early 1980s

July 1951

9th Anti-McCarthyite author Dashiell Hammett is jailed for 6 months for contempt of court. US Senator McCarthy is responsible for the Communist 'witch-hunt' currently taking place in the US. Hammett's novels include *The Maltese Falcon.*

9th The UK gets its **first all-electronic** computer when the Ferranti Mark I is installed at Manchester University.

The UK's first all-electronic computer

20th The 30-year rule of King Abdullah of Jordan ends when he is shot in the back outside one of Islam's holiest shrines, the Mosque of Omar, in Jerusalem. The fatal bullet is fired by a member of an opposition organisation. Guards shoot the culprit dead.

King Abdullah just before his assassination

August 1951

14th American newspaper tycoon William Hearst dies. Hearst was the inspiration for Orson Welles's *Citizen Kane.*

15th Austrian pianist Arthur Schnabel dies. Schnabel was renowned for his treatments of Beethoven, Mozart and Schubert.

21st The final toll puts the number of deaths at 132, after hurricane winds lash Jamaica, causing devastation.

30th A US Douglas Skyrocket shatters the absolute altitude record whilst flying over 1,000 mph (1,600 kmh) at an altitude of 13.7 miles (21.92 km).

September 1951

Ice cream van chimes are heard for the first time in the UK.

Japan's Prime Minister Shigeru Yoshida signs the Peace Treaty

8th A peace treaty signed by Japan and 48 other nations finally draws a line under the Second World War. Future rearmament by Japan is banned under the terms of the treaty, but the Soviet Foreign Minister still attacks the penalty clause as too lenient.

9th **Chinese troops** occupy Lhasa, the capital of Tibet.

16th **Thunderous applause** greets American actress Tallulah Bankhead, star of the film *Lifeboat*, as she appears at the London Palladium.

23rd **King George VI** has his left lung removed in a two-hour operation.

King George VI photographed in 1948

October 1951

Bell Telephone Laboratories' 'lineless' telephone

After their invention in 1948, transistors are used for the first time in a commercial telephone system. ☢

4th Vincent Minnelli's *An American In Paris*, starring Gene Kelly, premieres in New York.

6th W. K. Kellogg, health fanatic and pioneer of the breakfast-cereal empire, dies.

16th Rock and Roller Little Richard makes his first recording for RCA after winning a talent contest. 🎶

1951 Books:

A Catcher in the Rye by J. D. Salinger
Day of the Triffids by John Wyndham

16th Ali Khan, Prime Minister of Pakistan, is killed by a Muslim assassin.

26th Churchill returns to Number 10, at the age of 77, after the Tories scrape an election win over the ruling Labour party.

31st The first specially designed pedestrian crossings are unveiled in the UK. The crossings are marked out by broad black-and-white stripes; not surprisingly they have been dubbed 'Zebra Crossings' by the public.

November 1951

A military coup takes place in Thailand, while the king is out of the country.

Tough Hollywood actor Robert Mitchum is involved in a pub brawl with a professional heavyweight boxer: Mitchum wins.

20th A mass evacuation from Suez, of British servicemen and their families, begins as violence continues in the Canal Zone between British troops and Egyptian police. The departure is seen as a victory in the fight to drive out the British forces.

28th A strange calm **descends** over war-torn Korea as a truce brings about an unofficial cease-fire.

Communist officers prepare to meet UN representatives

December 1951

4th **Fierce fighting** erupts in Suez in a new wave of anti-British riots.

24th **The independent federation** of Libya is founded – the first independent state to be created by the United Nations, in accordance with its 1949 regulations. The ruler of the new nation is King Idris III.

26th *The African Queen*, starring Humphrey Bogart and Katherine Hepburn, opens in New York.

29th **A rocket, carrying a crew of monkeys**, has returned safely to earth. The US sent the converted V2 rocket into space for just a few minutes. All four monkeys have survived.

1952

January 1952

1st **The new GCE school exam** gets a bad report from headmasters, who claim pupils find it too hard.

2nd **Cecil B. de Mille's** *The Greatest Show On Earth*, starring James Stewart, opens in Hollywood.

12th **The prototype of the new** *Valiant*, Britain's first bomber able to carry nuclear weapons, crashes during a test flight.

21st **A new report predicts** that the Leaning Tower of Pisa will collapse in 2151. It leans an extra millimetre each year, according to the study. ☢

South Africa continues
to pass new Apartheid-led laws.

24th India stages its first International Film Festival.
Films from 21 countries are shown.

26th Rampaging **mobs** murder 17 British people in a night of violence, looting and fire-raising in the Egyptian capital of Cairo. Many burn to death in the city's favourite nightspot for rich Britons, the Turf Club; Barclays Bank, the bank of most ex-patriates, is also targetted by arsonists.

February 1952

6th Britain goes into mourning after King George VI dies in his sleep at Sandringham. His daughter Elizabeth becomes Queen Elizabeth II. She flies back to London from Kenya and cancels her forthcoming tour of Australia and New Zealand.

12th In their first home Test against the West Indies, New Zealand lose by five wickets.

20th Janet Attwegg takes the gold for Britain in the figure-skating event at the Winter Olympics.

21st American actress Elizabeth Taylor weds Michael Wilding.

Portrait of the new Queen, 1952

UK identity cards are scrapped, 13 years after being introduced at the start of the Second World War.

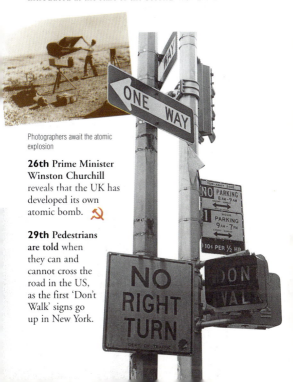

Photographers await the atomic explosion

26th Prime Minister **Winston Churchill** reveals that the UK has developed its own atomic bomb.

29th Pedestrians are told when they can and cannot cross the road in the US, as the first 'Don't Walk' signs go up in New York.

March 1952

1st Jawaharlal Nehru wins India's first elections.

8th In Philadelphia, a mechanical heart is used for the first time. The device keeps the patient, a 41-year-old male, alive for 80 minutes while he receives heart surgery. Sadly, the patient dies later due to unrelated causes.

A breakthrough in cardiac treatment

10th Former president, Fulgencio Batistá, overthrows the current Cuban government.

21st Kwame Nkrumah is **elected Prime Minister** of the Gold Coast – the first African Prime Minister south of the Sahara.

Jawaharlal Pandit Nehru addressing his people

April 1952

9th The Queen says the royal family will keep the surname Windsor.

The Nevada desert explosion

15th President Truman officially ends the war in the Pacific by signing a multi-nation treaty recognising Japanese sovereignty.

22nd
The most powerful atomic bomb yet tested has been detonated in the Nevada desert. The test was extensively covered by TV networks and attracted an audience of over 35 million throughout the US.

May 1952

First passengers board the BOAC Comet

2nd The new UK jet airliner, Comet, makes its first scheduled flight. The aircraft departs from London for

Johannesburg carrying 36 passengers. BOAC, the plane's operators, expect the journey to take 18 hours 40 minutes, including refuelling stops.

6th Italian educationalist and nursery pioneer, Maria Montessori, dies at the age of 82. Her first school was opened in Rome in 1907. Since then her name and teaching methods have become famous throughout the world.

Italian educationalist Maria Montessori

1952 Books:

The Old Man and the Sea by Ernest Hemingway
Invisible Man by Ralph Ellison
East of Eden by John Steinbeck

8th The UN forces make a surprise dawn raid on North Korea, using bombs and napalm.

10th Orson Welles's *Othello* wins the Grand Prix at the International Festival of Film in Cannes.

16th The US company Bell launch the first mechanical telephone answering machines.

20th Eight regions throughout Scotland and England have been designated to become nature reserves.

Ernest Hemingway relaxes on holiday

June 1952

The *Goon Show* starts broadcasting.

5th Yorkshire bowler, Freddie Trueman, takes seven wickets in his Test match debut at Headingley, Leeds.

14th The *USS Nautilus*, the world's first nuclear-powered submarine, undergoes tests in the US.

15th *The Diary of Anne Frank* is published. It is a harrowing, first-hand account of a German-Jewish family's wartime struggles in Holland. It chronicles their desperate attempt to evade capture by the Nazis by hiding in an attic for two years.

The *USS Nautilus*

Die is een foto, zoals
ik me zou wensen,
altijd zo te zijn.
Dan had ik nog wel
een kans om naar
Holywood te komen.

Anne Frank.
0 Oct. 1942

Anne Frank and diary extract

17th
The British
ferry *Lord Warden* goes into
service. It is of a radical
new design allowing
cars to drive straight on
and off. The Roll-on
Roll-Off, or 'Ro Ro' as it has been christened, will operate
on the busy Dover-Boulogne route.

20th The government
announces the introduction
of blinking orange beacons
for zebra crossings. They
become known as 'Belisha
beacons' after the Minister
of Transport.

Modern 'Ro-Ro' ferry

26th A peaceful protest
against Apartheid laws is launched
in South Africa by blacks and other coloured races.

July 1952

2nd Jewellery worth £3,000 is stolen from Elizabeth Taylor's hotel room in London.

5th The last tram leaves London's streets. It ran from Woolwich to New Cross.

5th Maureen 'Little Mo' Connelly wins the Wimbledon Ladies' singles title at the first attempt.

Midnight crowds say farewell to the last tram in Streatham

7th The American liner *United States* sets a new record time for crossing the Atlantic. Taking 3 days, 10 hours and 40 minutes, it travels at an average speed of 35.59 knots to win the coveted Blue Riband.

The President's daughter, Margaret Truman, aboard *United States*

11th General Dwight D. Eisenhower runs for President with Richard Nixon as his Republican running mate.

16th Motoring reaches new levels of comfort when General Motors introduces air-conditioning on some models.

Dwight Eisenhower photographed in 1955

26th Argentine politician Eva Perón dies aged 33. Evita, as she was popularly known, started out as a night-club singer. After becoming First Lady of Argentina she fought to legalise divorce and promote the rights of women and the poor. The rule of Perón and her husband was also notable for a rise in corruption, torture and disappearances.

26th In the US, Adlai Stevenson is chosen as the new Democratic candidate.

Eva Perón, First Lady of Argentina

August 1952

The fringe is back for the autumn and the elfin look of Audrey Hepburn and the stars of the film *Jules et Jim* is much copied. Hemlines continue to get shorter.

The flip-top cigarette packet is patented in the US.

At the Olympic Games, Emil Zapotek wins the 5,000 metres, the 10,000 metres and the marathon; his wife, Dana Zapotek, wins the javelin event.

11th Harrow schoolboy Crown Prince Hussein becomes King of Jordan in place of his father, King Talal, who has been diagnosed schizophrenic.

16th Freak **floods** course through the coastal Devon village of Lynmouth killing 45 and leaving thousands homeless.

The Oval, the home of championship cricket

22nd Surrey win the **County Cricket Championship** for first time since 1914.

26th A UK Canberra **bomber** crosses the Atlantic twice in just seven hours and 59 minutes.

30th The Geodesic dome is invented by R. Buckminster Fuller. The dome offers huge strength and weight advantages over traditional buildings.

September 1952

6th A prototype jet crashes at Farnborough Air Show, killing the 2 pilots and 26 spectators, just seconds after breaking the sound barrier.

Helping the injured at Farnborough

10th The West German government agrees to pay 3,450 million marks (about £287 million) in compensation to the Israelis, for Nazi persecution of Jews during the Second World War. Payments will be made in regular annual instalments over the next 14 years.

23rd Freddie Trueman wins the Cricket Writers' Club award for the Young Player of the Year.

Freddie Trueman acknowledges the applause at Edgbaston

23rd Hollywood's greatest clown, Charlie Chaplin, makes his first visit home to London, since 1929.

29th John Cobb, holder of the world land-speed record, is killed in a jet-powered boat on Loch Ness, whilst attempting the same on water.

John Cobb's *Crusader* prior to his record attempt

30th The first film shot in the 'Cinerama' format is released. The format gives audiences a 180° screen.

Agatha Christie's play *The Mousetrap* opens in the West End in 1952. In 1974, it takes the record as the world's longest-running play.

October 1952

3rd **Following an announcement** earlier in the year, the UK detonates its first atomic bomb. The test is carried out in the remote Monte Bello islands off north-western Australia. The blast is visible over 160km (100miles) away. ☢☢

3rd **Tea rationing** in the UK comes to an end.

The British tradition of High Tea is revived

Nuclear-powered batteries used in tiny, lifesaving, pacemakers

4th **The pacemaker,** a device for regulating heartbeats, is fitted to a patient in the US. The electronic device emulates the heart's own natural pacemaker, and is a vital breakthrough in the treatment of heart disease. ☢☢

Bill and Ben The Flowerpot Men make their first appearance on UK television in 1952.

Bill and Ben in the 1970's

8th A rail crash claims 112 lives in a horrific three-train pile-up at Harrow station.

Mangled train coaches litter Harrow station

9th David Lean's drama documentary film, *The Sound Barrier*, opens at the Empire Theatre, Leicester Square.

20th British soldiers fly into Kenya to help quell an uprising by Mau Mau terrorists.

November 1952

5th 'Ike' Eisenhower sweeps to White House victory with a record popular vote in the presidential election.

Weizmann being sworn in as Israel's President

9th Israel's first President, the world-famous chemist Chaim Weizmann, dies at home.

9th At London's Royal Opera House, the new star soprano, Maria Callas, receives a standing ovation after her impressive, if occasionally shrill, debut in the difficult leading role in Bellini's opera, *Norma*.

14th *NME* publishes the first pop-singles chart.

30th After its first test on 6 November, the US has detonated another H-bomb on the tiny island of Eniwetok in the South Pacific. Estimates of the blast put it as the largest yet by far.

Maria Callas at home in Paris

December 1952

London smog causes over 2,000 deaths due to high pollution levels.

The world digests news of the first person to undergo a male-to-female sex change operation and go public. Ex-GI George Jorgensen becomes Christine Jorgensen, thanks to a combination of surgery and hormone treatment by a Danish surgical team led by Christian Hamburger.

29th The first transistorised hearing aids are manufactured in the US by the Sontone Corp.

Transistorised hearing aid

1953

January 1953

Dr Frederick Sanger establishes the molecular structure of the hormone insulin. It will help to start the manufacture of insulin for the treatment of diabetes. In 1958, this discovery earns Dr Sanger a Nobel Prize.

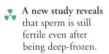

A new study reveals that sperm is still fertile even after being deep-frozen.

1st Influential country music singer Hank Williams dies of heart failure.

Rita Hayworth

3rd Samuel Beckett's play, *Waiting for Godot*, is lauded by the critics at its Paris premiere.

Waiting For Godot at the Theatre Royal, Stratford East

14th Vaughan Williams's *Symphonia Antarctica*, conducted by Sir John Barborolli, premieres at Manchester's Free Trade Hall.

27th US actress and dancer Rita Hayworth divorces Prince Aly Khan, son of the Aga Khan.

28th Teenager Derek Bentley hangs at Wandsworth Prison for the murder of a policeman in a failed robbery. In 1998, Bentley receives a posthumous pardon.

31st The Irish Sea claims 128 lives as a ferry sinks near Stranraer – open cargo doors allow water to flood in. 44 people survive.

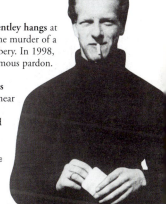

Prisoner Derek Bentley awaits sentence

February 1953

1st Hollywood reveals that 20th Century Fox intends to convert its entire movie-making operation to the new, wide-screen technique of CinemaScope, which was invented by Frenchman Henri Chrétien. The first CinemaScope film will be *The Robe*.

1st RAF Squadron No. 194 becomes active in Singapore; it is the UK's first helicopter unit.

3rd Dutch dykes burst causing major flooding and the loss of more than 1,000 lives.

Aerial view of flooded Goedereede, Holland

1953 Books:

Casino Royale by Ian Fleming
Fahrenheit 451 by Ray Bradbury
The Long Goodbye by Raymond Chandler

3rd **Sea defences** from Lincolnshire to Kent are destroyed as strong winds and high tides batter England's east coast. More than 280 are feared drowned and many thousands lose their homes.

5th **Britain's children** celebrate as sweet rationing comes to an end.

25th Leonard Bernstein's musical comedy *Wonderful Town*, starring Rosalind Russell, opens at Madison Square Garden.

Leonard Bernstein photographed in 1969

Rowing boats rescue flood victims at Whitstable

Arthur Miller's play *The Crucible* has its first performance.

March 1953

IBM delivers its first Model 701 computer. The new machine goes to the Los Alamos nuclear-research centre, where details of its work remain top secret.

Actress Vivien Leigh enters hospital after suffering a nervous breakdown while filming.

5th Joseph Stalin, leader of the USSR, dies at the age of 73, four days after suffering a brain haemorrhage. Stalin caused countless deaths in his relentless bid to stamp out internal opposition during his 30-year hold on the country.

5th The French Fauvist artist Raoul Dufy dies almost a year after winning the Venice Bienniel. The Fauves (from the French for 'wild animals') experimented with strong colours and brush techniques producing richly dynamic pictures unlike any previous artistic group.

Russian leaders flank Stalin's coffin

5th Composer Sergei Prokofiev dies.

13th After 28 years, Eisenstein's *The Battleship Potemkin* finally goes on general release in France. The film, based on the start of the Russian Revolution, has been banned until now.

20th The RAF uses helicopters in combat for the first time, airlifting troops in Malaya.

25th The grim discovery of bodies behind the walls in London's Rillington Place prompts a manhunt for homeowner John Christie.

Poster advertising *The Battleship Potemkin*

John Christie and his Rillington Place house

April 1953

8th Head of the Mau Mau terrorist organisation in Kenya, Jomo 'Burning Spear' Kenyatta, is sentenced to seven years hard labour for running the murderous attacks on farms owned by European settlers.

Kenyatta escorted from court in handcuffs

16th **The Queen launches** the new royal yacht, *Britannia*, built in Glasgow.

The much-loved puppet Sooty is seen on UK television for the first time in 1953.

17th Charlie Chaplin announces he will never return to the US where he has lived for the last 40 years. Chaplin, star of dozens of silent films, was accused of being a Communist and could face legal action if he returns. He has now settled in Switzerland.

Charlie Chaplin visits a Swiss vineyard

25th The 'double-helix' structure of DNA, the chemical that 'makes us what we are', is worked out by doctors James Watson and Francis Crick. This begins a scientific understanding of genetic codes. ☢

27th Crucial talks begin in Cairo between the UK and Egypt on the future of the Suez canal zone. ☭

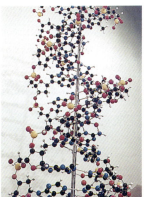

29th The first experimental 3-D television transmissions take place in Los Angeles. In the same month the first TV guide is published in the US. ☢

Laboratory model of a DNA molecule

May 1953

1st The torment is finally over for 22 British prisoners of war flown home from Korea. The war began in June 1950.

2nd A UK Comet jet airliner crashes killing all 43 people aboard. The accident occurred during a violent tropical storm just north of Calcutta, India, but there is concern that both wings seem to have sheared off the aircraft prior to hitting the ground.

2nd 100,000 fans watch Stanley Matthews steer Blackpool to a 4–3 FA Cup Final victory over Bolton.

15th In the US, Rocky Marciano defeats Jersey Joe Walcott to retain his world heavyweight boxing title.

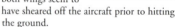

1953 sees French artist
Henri Matisse exhibit *The Snail*.

Hugh Heffner's *Playboy* reaches
magazine stands for the first time.

18th Jacqueline Cochrane becomes the first woman to
fly faster than the speed of sound.

29th Edmund Hillary and Sherpa Tensing conquer the
tallest mountain on Earth. The pair reach the top of
Everest at 11:30 a.m. and spend just 15 minutes on the
summit before making their way back down.

Members of the Everest expedition arrive in London

June 1953

2nd Queen Elizabeth II is crowned. It is the first televised royal coronation and is watched by millions of people around the world. The Queen travels to Westminster Abbey in her golden ceremonial carriage. It is pulled by eight grey horses.

4th Joseph Mankiewiczs's screen version of *Julius Caesar*, starring Marlon Brando, premieres in Hollywood.

8th Benjamin Britten's opera, *Gloriana* (to celebrate the Coronation of Queen Elizabeth II), premieres in London.

30th Carbonless copy paper is patented in the US by the NCR corporation.

Marlon Brando relaxes away from the big screen

July 1953

15th The film *Gentleman Prefer Blondes* opens in New York. It stars Marilyn Monroe and Jane Russell.

Portrait of the author Hilaire Belloc

16th Hilaire Belloc dies aged 82. The son of a French barrister, Belloc became a naturalised Englishman in 1902 and a Liberal MP in 1906. A committed Roman Catholic he was known for his children's books, such as *The Bad Child's Book of Beasts*, his cautionary tales, travel and religious writing.

26th Cuban revolutionary Fidel Castro is imprisoned after attempting to overthrow Batistá's government.

27th The Korean War ends after three years and more than two million deaths.

US troops in action in Korea

August 1953

5th Director Fred Zinnemann's film version of James Jones's novel *From Here To Eternity* opens in the US. Its main stars are Burt Lancaster and Frank Sinatra.

5th The first all-electronic concert takes place – the RCA synthesiser plays *Chopin's Opus 53*.

7th Two million French state workers walk out in a national strike called by the unions over the government's economic proposals, including the raising of retirement age. All transport, gas and electricity supplies, as well as public services, grind to a halt at the height of holiday season.

French streets left littered due to strike

The first open-heart operation is performed.

13th Disaster strikes the Greek Ionian Islands where earthquakes and tidal waves are reported to have caused more than 1,000 deaths and left 100,000 people homeless.

1953 sees the first pregnancy
made possible by frozen sperm.

19th After 20 years of trying, England's cricketers finally win back the Ashes from Australia.

An RAF Hawker Hunter
takes off

31st An RAF Hawker Hunter jet fighter sets a new air-speed record of 1193.33 km/h (741.66 mph).

Crowds cheer England
and Australia's captains
at the Oval

September 1953

Ultra-high stiletto heels are the latest fashion in footwear for British women.

9th The ground-breaking **Parallel of Life and Art** exhibition opens at the ICA Gallery in London.

12th Senator John Kennedy marries Jacqueline Bouvier, a newspaper photographer, at a high-society ceremony.

28th The Ford company has revealed two new models for the European market. The Anglia and Prefect models represent the leading edge of smaller car design and feature many innovations, not least being available in a number of bright new colours.

Ford Anglia, marketed as the perfect family car

October 1953

8th British contralto Kathleen Ferrier dies from cancer aged 41. Her opera career lasted just seven years.

18th Protests in Poland as the religious leader Cardinal Wyszynski is arrested.

23rd Over 12 villages in southern Italy suffer major flood damage after heavy rains.

British opera singer Kathleen Ferrier

26th The Football Association celebrates its 90th year with a match between the Rest of the World and England at Wembley. Thanks to a last-gasp penalty from England's Alf Ramsey the match ends in a 4-4 draw.

November 1953

9th While undertaking a lecture tour of the US, the Welsh poet and writer, Dylan Thomas, dies at the Chelsea Hotel in New York. His death, at the age of 39, was brought about by years of heavy drinking. His works include *Under Milk Wood*.

Poet and writer Dylan Thomas

13th The British government gives commercial TV the go-ahead. It will be funded by advertisements.

25th England are given a footballing lesson as they lose 3–6 to Hungary at Wembley.

27th Playwright Eugene O'Neill dies at the age of 65.

Jubilant Hungarians celebrate their footballing victory

December 1953

10th Sir Winston Churchill is awarded the Nobel Prize for Literature for his historical works.

23rd Russian ex-security chief Lavrenti Beria is executed as a Western spy after a secret trial.

31st A group of scientists from the UK has arrived in Nepal with plans finally to discover the secret of the Yeti. Also known as the Abominable Snow Man, this mythical beast has suddenly become a *cause célèbre* after several footprints were discovered during a recent mountaineering expedition.

Mount Everest, where the Yeti is believed to live

1954

January 1954

The first clinical tests of a new female contraceptive commence in the US. A simple pill, containing the hormones progesterone and oestrogen, is taken once a day and appears to offer close to a 100 per cent success rate.

1st **Flashing direction indicator lights** become legal on motor vehicles in the UK.

2nd **Television can damage family life**, warns Pope Pius XII.

8th **US President Eisenhower** raises the question of whether the voting age should be lowered to 18. The answer is yes.

14th **Hollywood star Marilyn Monroe** marries baseball maestro Joe DiMaggio in San Francisco.

The Bell Telephone Laboratory develops the world's first solar battery.

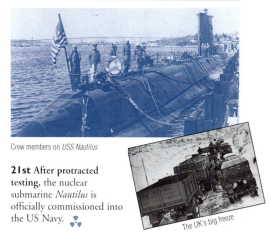

Crew members on *USS Nautilus*

21st After protracted testing, the nuclear submarine *Nautilus* is officially commissioned into the US Navy.

The UK's big freeze

31st The big freeze claims 23 lives as icy roads cause motoring mayhem across the UK.

UEFA (Union of European Football Associations) is established in 1954.

February 1954

5th *Lucky Jim*, Kingsley Amis's comic novel about a frustrated college lecturer, is published in the UK.

28th Dylan Thomas's radio play *Under Milk Wood* receives its first London reading, at the Old Vic.

12th A report by UK scientists claims definite links between smoking and lung cancer.

15th The 800th episode of radio soap opera *The Archers* is broadcast. It now has an audience of 10 million.

Actor Desmond Reynolds in *Under Milk Wood*

Kingsley Amis meditates at home

The Archers stars Bob Arnold and Courtney Hope

18th US Senator Joseph **McCarthy's** Permanent Subcommittee on Investigations homes in on the US Army in a hunt for supposed Communist sympathisers.

22nd Indian Prime Minister Nehru calls for peace between the French and the Communist Viet Minh in Indochina.

23rd US evangelist Billy Graham starts a three-month tour of the UK. He accepted the invitation from over 1,000 churches to bring his crusade across the Atlantic for an unpaid schedule of speaking engagements. He denies his mission is to 'save England' or tell people what to do.

Billy Graham attracts a crowd in Trafalgar Square

March 1954

21st Diplomat Kim Philby is recalled to London for questioning by MI6 over the Burgess-MacLean spy ring.

22nd Gold sells at $35 an ounce as the London Gold Market trades for the first time since 1939.

22nd The crew of a Japanese fishing boat are burnt by radiation from the US H-bomb test at Bikini Atoll.

27th Royal Tan wins the Grand National in which four horses die. The disaster, on the notoriously difficult circuit at Liverpool's Aintree race-course, prompts an inquiry by the RSPCA.

Diplomat Kim Philby in London

April 1954

4th Fearing that his failing memory may be affecting his working ability, 87-year-old Italian conductor Arturo Toscanini retires. His final concert was with the NBC Symphony Orchestra at Carnegie Hall.

9th The Comet airliner has been grounded for extensive tests after another crashes in the Mediterranean, killing all 21 on board.

10th French cinema pioneer Auguste Lumière, who patented his camera and projector design in 1895, dies.

18th Egypt has a new Prime Minister, Colonel Nasser – he took power by force.

May 1954

3rd The first pre-recorded stereo tapes go on sale in the UK featuring the Philharmonia Orchestra and the London Mozart Players.

6th Oxford medical student Roger Bannister becomes the first person to break the four-minute mile.

7th French forces are defeated at Dien Bien Phu by the Vietnamese. This is the end of French rule in Indochina.

14th The US Boeing Corporation unveils its first jet airliner, the 707.

14th **Nationalist China** drops out of the 1956 Melbourne Olympics after Communist China is allowed in.

17th **Blacks and whites must learn together** is the landmark decision made by the US Supreme Court. It makes racial segregation in state schools illegal, after concluding that the 1896 ruling that education should be 'separate but equal' is actually 'inherently unequal'.

The European Convention of Human Rights comes into force.

26th **Mau Mau terrorists** burn down Kenya's world-famous Tree Tops Hotel. It was here that Queen Elizabeth II received the news of her father's death in 1952.

Tree Tops hotel, Kenya

June 1954

2nd A coalition government, led by John Costello, takes over the Irish government from the Fianna Fail party.

2nd Lester Piggott wins the Derby on Never Say Die. At 18 he is the youngest-ever jockey to win the race.

10th Edith Sitwell and Somerset Maugham receive birthday honours from the Queen.

11th Iris Murdoch makes her debut with the novel *Under The Net*.

John Costello, Ireland's new leader

Author Iris Murdoch

1954 Films:

East of Eden
Rear Window
Seven Samurai

21st Australian athlete John Landy sets a new record of 3 min 58 secs for the mile.

25th Doctors say drink-drive tests should be stricter than the existing tests, which involve tongue twisters and walking in a straight line. Driving is becoming more accessible – manufacturers like Austin, Standard and Ford are all competing to build the UK'S cheapest car – and doctors are concerned that the current laws will prove ineffective if more people take to the road.

27th The Soviets claim to have constructed their first viable nuclear power station.

The future of drink-driving tests

July 1954

1st Myxomatosis has now all but destroyed the rabbit population in the UK. The fatal disease is highly infectious and agonising, causing swelling and skin tumours.

3rd Housewives ceremonially tear up their ration books in Trafalgar Square as 14 years of rationing comes to an end. Meat was the last rationed item and the National Association of Housewives say they will protest if prices fail to fall.

London housewives celebrate in Trafalgar Square

UK comedian Tony Hancock begins broadcasting
his radio programme *Hancock's Half Hour*.

5th Daily news bulletins start on British TV with the
BBC News.

9th Australian golfer **Peter
Thomson** takes the British Open
title with a round of 71.

15th The Boeing 707, unveiled
in May, makes its maiden flight.

**19th Mississippi-born
singer Elvis Presley** records
his first single 'That's all
right Mama'.

**21st The eight-year
Indochina war** between
French and Communist
forces ends with a pact
dividing Vietnam in half.

Peter Thompson winner of the Open Golf Championship

Switzerland are the football World Cup hosts.
The competition is won by Germany.

August 1954

4th The prototype of the UK's first supersonic jet fighter, the *Lightning*, takes to the air for the first time.

10th Champion jockey Sir Gordon Richards retires from racing. He has ridden 4,870 winners.

24th US President Eisenhower signs a bill making membership of the Communist Party illegal in the US, in a move aimed at putting pressure on the nation's Communist-influenced unions.

26th The first book of J. R. R. Tolkien's Middle Earth trilogy, *The Fellowship of the Ring*, is published in the UK.

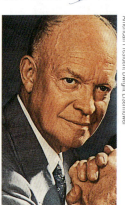

American President Dwight Eisenhower

September 1954

9th An earthquake-ravaged Algerian town vanishes in just 12 seconds, with 1,000 feared dead.

19th Naturist organisation the Federation of British Sun Clubs holds its first annual meeting. Naturism gathered momentum in Germany after the First World War and started to take off in the UK in the 1930s. The early 1950s has seen the formation of many more clubs.

25th Actress Audrey Hepburn, who won an Academy Award for *Roman Holiday*, marries Mel Ferrer.

October 1954

5th Marilyn Monroe sues Joe DiMaggio for divorce. She blames conflicting career demands.

6th Benjamin Britten's adaptation of Henry James's *The Turn of the Screw* premieres in the UK.

8th US troops help thousands of refugees reach South Vietnam as the Communist Viet Minh take over Hanoi.

Composer Benjamin Britten

Evacuees from North Vietnam flee from Hanoi

Author William Golding

15th *Lord of the Flies*, William Golding's savage story of shipwrecked English schoolboys going native on a desert island, is published in the UK. The book's examination of the group's reversion to primal behaviour is an allegory of the way that all humans behave in extreme situations.

19th Extensive studies point to metal fatigue as being the cause of the Comet crashes.

19th Talks between the UK and Egypt end in accord over the future of the Suez canal zone. Both sides sign the Anglo-Egyptian agreement, which will see a complete withdrawal of British troops from the area within 20 months.

November 1954

3rd The French painter Henri Matisse dies, after a long illness, aged 89. Matisse founded the groundbreaking Fauvist movement, which also included Dufy, Derain, Vlaminck and Kees Van Dongen. His works include *La Danse*, *The Red Studio* and *The Dinner Table (Harmony in Red)*.

19th American entertainer Sammy Davis Junior loses an eye in a car accident.

23rd General Motors produce their 50 millionth car – a gold-plated Chevrolet coupé.

29th The National Cancer Institute claims it has definite proof of a link between smoking and lung cancer. Tobacco companies hotly deny the research and threaten legal action.

December 1954

2nd US Senator Joe McCarthy is publicly censured for his allegations made in 1950, about Communists infiltrating the State Department.

8th The government publishes the Road Traffic Bill, which proposes introducing parking meters and MOTs. Meters will be confined to the Metropolitan Police district at first, while motor vehicle excise licences are only likely to be issued to cars that have passed a road-worthiness test.

9th Roger Bannister retires from athletics.

10th Ernest Hemingway wins the Nobel Prize for Literature. His works include *A Farewell to Arms*.

Author Ernest Hemingway on a fishing trip

1955

January 1955

Radar sets are introduced along the UK's roads to catch speeding motorists.

1st The Vickers Valiant enters service with the RAF, as the only UK aircraft able to carry atomic bombs.

10th Marian Anderson, an American contralto who received her musical education in the Choir of the Union Baptist Church in Philadelphia, becomes the first black person to sing at the Metropolitan Opera House in New York. She stars as Ulrica in Verdi's *Masked Ball*.

Marian Anderson signs her contract with the Metropolitan Opera

21st Scientists expose the Piltdown Man remains as a hoax. The bones, which were discovered in 1912, were claimed to have been the so-called 'Missing Link' in humanity's fossil record. In fact they are gorilla remains suitably stained to make them look old.

25th The USSR finally recognises the end of the war with Germany.

27th Michael Tippett's opera *Midsummer Marriage*, conducted by John Pritchard and starring Joan Sutherland, opens in London.

Composer Sir Michael Tippett

February 1955

HMS Ark Royal, the UK's largest-ever aircraft carrier, is completed.

2nd The British government unveils plans to invest £212 million on updating the road network over the next four years with new motorways stretching the length of England, and bypasses to ease congestion in major towns.

Georgi Malenkov photographed in 1956

8th The First Secretary of the Communist Party, Nikita Khrushchev, forces Soviet leader Georgi Malenkov's resignation.

8th London is to have a new tube line. It will run from Victoria to Walthamstow.

> Dorothy Hodgkinson discovers the composition of vitamin B12 in 1955.

10th **6,000 blacks** are forcibly evicted from Sophiatown, South Africa – the area has been designated for white residential use.

14th **The Tate Gallery,** which was founded in 1897 by the inventor of the sugar cube, Sir Henry Tate, finally shakes off its status as a subordinate part of the National Gallery. Instead it becomes an independent institution under the Tate Gallery Act. It will display modern British art.

Maureen Connolly, aged 20, in her wedding dress

22nd Maureen 'Little Mo' Connolly, retires from tennis and says she plans to get married.

London's Tate Gallery

March 1955

British bandleader Johnny Dankworth refuses to go to South Africa because of the country's colour-bar policy – turning down £10,000 in the process. He backs Father Trevor Huddlestone's call for entertainers to boycott South Africa.

Christian Dior

Johnny Dankworth with his wife, Cleo Laine

On the Waterfront sweeps the board at the Oscars.

1st Pioneering French fashion designer Christian Dior launches the A-line skirt.

1955 Books:

Lolita by Vladimir Nabokov
Moonraker by Ian Fleming

Sir Alexander Fleming
in his laboratory

11th Nobel prize-winning scientist, Sir Alexander Fleming, dies aged 74.

12th US jazz musician Charlie 'Bird' **Parker**, saxophonist, composer and bandleader, dies.

20th Director Richard Brooks's version of Evan Hunter's novel, *The Blackboard Jungle*, opens in New York.

24th In the US, the curtain goes up on Tennessee Williams's play, *Cat On A Hot Tin Roof.*

28th The Israeli army raids the Egyptian-held Gaza Strip, leaving 42 dead. It is the first attack since the 1949 armistice.

The film version of *Cat On A Hot Tin Roof*

April 1955

3rd 300 are feared dead after a train crashes in Mexico.

3rd Representatives from eight footballing nations meet in Paris to set up football's European Cup competition.

The modern face of European football

5th Sir Winston Churchill stands down as Prime Minister at the age of 80, but stays on as a backbencher.

Winston Churchill with his successor, Sir Anthony Eden

12th Clinical trials prove the efficacy of the Salk Polio vaccine. Widespread vaccinations will follow.

15th The first McDonalds restaurant opens. It is in the town of Des Plaines, Illinois.

Stocks of the polio vaccine for immunisation campaigns

18th German-born physicist Albert Einstein dies; the creator of the Theory of Special Relativity (1905) and the Theory of General Relativity (1915). A Jew, Einstein left Germany for the US when Hitler's Nazi Party came to power. Einstein was influential in America's decision to build an atomic bomb, although he later spoke out against nuclear weapons.

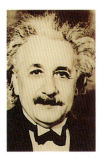

21st Two missing English schoolboys are found murdered in Kenya by Mau Mau terrorists.

26th The Bandung conference – the first meeting of 'non-aligned' African and Asian countries – closes.

May 1955

1st Stirling Moss becomes the first Briton to win the Mille Miliga road race in Italy.

Stirling Moss in his winning Mercedes

4th Yorkshire and England cricketer Len Hutton is made an honorary member of the MCC.

6th The UK is in dispute with Argentina and Chile over ownership of the Falkland Islands.

Len Hutton with his wife and sons

Hiroshima after the blast

8th Some of the Hiroshima **victims**, horribly burnt in the blast, are given plastic surgery in California.

14th A new military alliance of Eastern-bloc nations is created as Soviet leader Bulganin signs the Warsaw Pact.

15th Austria is finally allowed independence from Germany – 10 years after the end of the Second World War.

27th Anthony Eden leads the Tories to a UK General Election win, with an increased majority.

28th 16 Teddy boys are **arrested** after a dance hall disturbance in Bath. Razor attacks and fights between gangs and against the police have grown in frequency in recent years. The term 'Teddy boy' was coined by the *Daily Express* in an article of September 1953.

June 1955

Gold-lamé-suited pianist Liberace is in the charts with his instrumental of 'Unchained Melody'.

2nd **Kachenjunga,** the world's third highest mountain, has been conquered by a team of UK climbers led by Charles Evans. Like the Everest expedition before it, the attempt was made possible by new developments in clothing and oxygen equipment.

6th Bill Haley's 'Rock Around the Clock' hits US number 1. The song was considered a dud only a few months ago but after appearing in *Blackboard Jungle,* a new movie about teenage delinquency at a New York High School, its popularity has soared.

Liberace in the 1970s

1955 Films:

*The Dam Busters • The Lady Killers
Panther Panchali • The Seven Year Itch*

11th 83 people are killed in a horrific accident at the Le Mans race track.

14th A pregnant woman is killed and hundreds are injured when lightning strikes Royal Ascot.

15th The US and UK agree to exchange information about atomic energy.

The atomic US submarine, *Nautilus*

July 1955

1st **A six-week national dock strike** ends as union leaders in the UK order a return to work.

6th **Richard Hamilton's** Man, Machine and Motion exhibition opens at London's ICA. ☢☢

7th **An experimental supersonic** version of the Hunter jet fighter crashes at the Farnborough Air Show. ☢

13th **Ruth Ellis hangs.** Ellis, 26, shot her lover David Blakely with a Smith and Wesson handgun in an uncontrollable fit of jealousy. The ex-model and mother-of-two is executed at Holloway prison less than a month after a jury finds her guilty of murder.

Ex-model and convicted murderer, Ruth Ellis

Total silence at the UK's inactive docks

Mickey Mouse in one of Disneyland's many parades

18th Walt Disney's theme park, Disneyland, opens in California – a 160-acre, $17 million fantasy land.

20th The US claims back the world air-speed record when a Super Sabre reaches 1323.03 km/h (822.27 mph).

23rd In the Lake District, Donald Campbell breaks the world water-speed record, travelling in *Bluebird* at 325.31 kmh (202.32 mph).

27th Smoke-control areas are created in the UK with the publication of the Clean Air Bill.

August 1955

4th **Figure-hugging blue jeans** are the number one selling style for women.

Samuel Beckett: author, playwright, poet and novelist

10th **Samuel Beckett's**, *Waiting for Godot*, directed by Peter Hall, is ridiculed by critics after its London premiere. This is in stark contrast to the enthusiastic reaction – 'a perfect example of the Theatre of the Absurd' – it received at its Paris premiere in January 1953.

12th **German writer Thomas Mann dies.** The Nobel Prize-winner's works included *Death in Venice*.

13th **Armed IRA terrorists** attempt to steal weapons from an army barracks in Arborfield, Berkshire. All five men are arrested.

The film version of Mann's *Death in Venice*

14th The Royal Academy Summer Exhibition, featuring Annigoni's portrait of Queen Elizabeth II, breaks all attendance records.

15th In a similar attack to that in Berkshire two days previously, five Irish terrorists, members of the IRA, hold up an army barracks in North Rhyl, Wales, in a bid to steal arms. Their plan fails after the soldiers pretend not to know the whereabouts of the armoury.

First UN troops arrive in Port Said, Egypt

31st Hopes are raised for an end to the Gaza hostilities, after the UN cease-fire terms are accepted by Egypt.

September 1955

18th **The Foreign Office** finally admits diplomats Burgess and MacLean were Soviet spies.

Soviet spies, Guy Burgess and Donald MacLean

22nd **Independent television** is launched in the UK. The first advert to appear is for SR Toothpaste.

26th **Birds Eye** introduce the 'Fish Finger' into the UK.

30th **Actor James Dean dies in a car crash aged 24.** He made just three films: *East of Eden, Rebel Without a Cause* and *Giant,* but already he had come to represent American youth's restlessness and purposelessness. After his death he becomes a cultural icon.

October 1955

EMI and Decca raise the price of singles from five shillings to 5s/7d.

The first transistorised radios are marketed in the US by Regency Electronics.

12th American swimmer **Florence Chadwick** swims the English Channel for the second time. Her mammoth feat takes 13 hours and 55 minutes.

16th James Dean's second **film**, *Rebel Without A Cause,* opens in the US 16 days after his death. His third film, *Giant*, also starring Rock Hudson and Elizabeth Taylor, was unfinished when he died, although all of Dean's scenes had been completed.

James Dean stars in *Rebel Without A Cause*

1955 UK TV Programmes:

The Benny Hill Show
Saturday Night At The Palladium
Dixon of Dock Green
Crackerjack

20th The BBC demonstrates the first UK colour television transmissions from Alexandra Palace. ☢

26th *The Village Voice*, the newspaper for the community of New York's Greenwich Village, is founded.

31st Princess Margaret calls off her marriage to Captain Peter Townsend, a divorced equerry to her late father.

Donald Campbell in his jet speedboat, *Bluebird*, in July 1955

November 1955

16th Donald Campbell sets a new world water-speed record in the US – 345.92 km/h (216.2 mph).

25th Black bus passenger Rosa Parks is arrested in Montgomery, Alabama, after she refuses to give up her seat for a white woman. 50,000 black protesters, led by Dr Martin Luther King, boycott buses and call for an end to segregation.

28th Cyprus declares a state of emergency after Greek terrorists kill five soldiers in a month.

30th The first floodlit international football match, England v. Spain, is played at Wembley. England win 4–1.

Cypriot NAAFI building after a firebomb

December 1955

Bill Haley: singer, musician and bandleader

Bill Haley releases 'See You Later Alligator' in the US.

3rd The UK and Egypt amend the 1953 agreement on Sudan to open the door to self-determination. Two long-time Sudanese political enemies are now calling on all the nation's politicians to work together on quickly creating an all-party government.

14th **Hugh Gaitskill** becomes leader of the Labour Party in the UK – a success for the right wing of the party.

19th **Carl Perkins** records 'Blue Suede Shoes' – based on someone's footwear he spotted while playing a concert.

29th **The Soviets** claim to have developed a ballistic missile with a range of 6,400 km (4,000 miles).

'Blue Suede Shoes' was one of many Juke Box favourites in the 50s

1956

January 1956

Prince Rainier of Monaco is to marry US actress Grace Kelly.

1st The independence of Sudan is announced officially.

2nd The Astronomer Royal declares that he does not believe humans will ever travel in space.

17th Plans are announced for the UK's new early warning system to cope with air attacks.

Prince Rainier and Princess Grace

17th It is proposed that the City of London will have a new arts complex, to be built in the Barbican area – at the cost of £55 million.

London's Barbican Centre houses theatres, restaurants and galleries

18th Author Alan Alexander Milne dies aged 74. He was educated at Westminster School and Trinity College, Cambridge, and later joined the staff of *Punch*. His most famous work, *Winnie The Pooh*, was written for his son Christopher Robin.

26th Britain imposes a total ban on the import and export of the drug heroin.

1956 sees the ordination of the first female Presbyterian minister, in the US.

February 1956

The UK's first yellow 'No Parking' lines appear on roads near Slough.

1st The Declaration of Washington is signed by President Eisenhower and Anthony Eden, as an affirmation of the US's and UK's joint policy in the Middle East.

21st The Duke of Edinburgh launches an award scheme for enterprising young people.

22nd The first UK floodlit football match (Portsmouth v. Newcastle) ends when the lights fuse.

22nd Elvis Presley enters the US charts for the first time with 'Heartbreak Hotel'. The young star was 'discovered' by Sun Records.

29th Ex-BBC star Muffin the Mule makes his debut on ITV.

March 1956

Recorded weather forecasts can now be accessed with a simple phone call.

Archbishop Makarios at Rome Airport

10th Riots in Cyprus break out after the British deport Greek Cypriot leader Archbishop Makarios.

10th An RAF Fairey Delta 2 shatters the air-speed record with a new record of 1,821.39 km/h (1,132 mph).

15th With a star-studded cast, including Julie Andrews and Rex Harrison, *My Fair Lady*, Lerner and Leowe's musical version of George Bernard Shaw's play *Pygmalion*, opens on the New York stage.

Audrey Hepburn, in the film version of *My Fair Lady*

English writer Laurie Lee publishes his semi-autobiographical novel, *Cider With Rosie*, in 1956.

17th The Bill Haley movie, *Rock Around The Clock*, opens to a riotous reception in British cinemas.

18th Soviet Communist chief Khrushchev launches a scathing attack on Stalin, branding him a brutal, criminal murderer.

24th Devon Loch slips and loses the Grand National – with just 50 yards to go.

April 1956

10th **Nat King Cole is attacked** on stage by six anti-rhythm and blues vigilantes.

18th **The UK welcomes** the USSR's Nikita Khrushchev, the First Secretary of the Soviet Communist Party, and Nikolai Bulganin on an historic eight-day visit.

19th **American actress Grace Kelly** weds Prince Rainier III, monarch of Monaco, in a televised service.

Nikita Khrushchev meets ballerina Beryl Grey

21st Rocky Marciano retires aged 33.
Marciano (real name Rocco
Marchegiano) worked in a shoe
factory and fought as an amateur
before turning pro in 1947. As
a professional he won all of his
49 fights and took the world
heavyweight boxing title on six
occasions.

29th The US claims that it can
build missiles capable of
flying between the
continents.

Rocky Marciano, world heavyweight
boxing champion

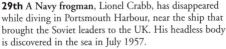

29th A Navy frogman, Lionel Crabb, has disappeared
while diving in Portsmouth Harbour, near the ship that
brought the Soviet leaders to the UK. His headless body
is discovered in the sea in July 1957.

The Soviet ship at Portsmouth

May 1956

1st A mass demonstration is held in Berlin by 100,000 committed supporters of the reunification of Germany.

5th Manchester City beats Birmingham City 3–1 in the FA Cup Final. It later transpires that Manchester's goalkeeper, Bert Trautmann, played with a broken neck.

11th Noted American astronomer Walter S. Adams dies. He is renowned for his exhaustive studies of sunspots as well as for his revelatory work on the white dwarf star Sirius B.

Bert Trautmann receives first aid

14th John Osborne's anti-establishment play *Look Back in Anger* opens at the Royal Court Theatre.

The Electron Microscope is developed
by Erwin Wilhelm Miller.

16th Jim Laker takes
all 10 opposition
wickets as Surrey
defeat the Australians
at the Oval.

21st The US has
dropped its first H-
bomb from an aircraft.
The test was carried out at the now much-battered
Bikini Atoll, and was deemed successful by the Pentagon.
Previous tests had been from ground-mounted bombs.

Mushroom cloud over Bikini Atoll

June 1956

13th The last British troops leave the Suez canal zone less than a week ahead of the 1954 agreement deadline.

13th In Paris, Real Madrid defeat Stade de Reims 4–3 to win the first European Cup.

22nd English poet Walter de la Mare dies.

28th In Poland, 38 people die during riots over inflation.

29th Marilyn Monroe marries playwright Arthur Miller. Pulitzer prize-winning Miller, who wrote *Death of a Salesman* and *The Crucible*, is sex symbol Monroe's unlikely third husband. Miller fell foul of the House Un-American Activities Committee earlier this year.

Israeli troops in Gaza

July 1956

10th A debate over the future of capital punishment in the UK continues after a vote in the House of Lords swings overwhelmingly against abolition. MPs in the Commons earlier backed retention of hanging for prisoners serving life who go on to commit murder.

26th The Electronic Random Number Indicator Equipment (ERNIE) goes on-line in London. It will choose the numbers for winning premium bonds.

Anti-hanging protesters outside Wandsworth Prison

Surrey bowler Jim Laker (centre)

27th Jim Laker takes 19 wickets in the fourth Test match against the Australians at Old Trafford.

August 1956

11th US artist Jackson Pollock dies. He was well known for his drip paintings on large canvasses.

16th Hungarian-born US actor **Bela Lugosi**, star of *Dracula* and *Plan 9 From Outer Space*, dies.

20th Calder Hall, the UK's **first atomic power station**  produces its first electricity. The station consists of four gas-cooled reactors and should be capable of producing 90,000 KW, as well as weapons-grade plutonium.

Actor Bela Lugosi
in the stage play of *Dracula*

Calder Hall nuclear power station, renamed
Windscale then Sellafield

The Whitechapel Art Gallery hosts its first Pop Art exhibition, This Is Tomorrow.

Michael Croft and students rehearse Henry V

27th Michael Croft, an actor, novelist and school teacher, sets up the National Youth Theatre to give talented young actors the chance to partake in professional productions of Shakespeare's plays during the school holidays.

30th Traffic wardens are to hit the UK's streets, to oversee new parking meters and to ease the police workload.

30th Colonel Nasser expels two British 'spies' – a move mirrored in London with Egyptian expulsions two days later.

September 1956

9th Elvis Presley appears on the US TV programme *The Ed Sullivan Show*, in front of an audience of up to 54 million. The 21-year-old's hip gyrations are so suggestive that his pelvis is being banned from future recordings – from now on Elvis will only be shown from the waist up.

25th A Transatlantic telephone cable laid between Oban (in Scotland) and Newfoundland takes its first call.

28th An agreement to re-establish full diplomatic relations is finally reached between Japan and the USSR.

October 1956

7th Clarence Birdseye, US frozen-food pioneer and register of 300 patents, dies.

26th Hungary demands freedom from Soviet rule. Demonstrators calling for independence, after 11 years under Moscow control, spark a national uprising with people taking on Soviet tanks and troops with their bare hands. The initial death toll is reportedly over 3,000.

Hungarians burn reminders of Soviet occupation

31st British and French troops launch an air raid on Suez to keep the canal open to international traffic.

Plan showing military manoeuvres around Suez

November 1956

6th Eisenhower wins his second term as US President with even bigger electoral backing than the first time. ☭

28th Controversy greets the Paris premiere of Roger Vadim's *And God Created Woman* – because of the film's explicit sexual content.

30th In a technological breakthrough, CBS broadcast the first network television show made using videotape for a delayed broadcast. Until now all network shows have been broadcast live. ☢

American President Dwight Eisenhower

December 1956

3rd Anglo-French troops pull out of Suez following the arrival of United Nations forces.

Cruise ships sail along the Suez canal

10th The International Monetary Fund agrees to provide a $1,300 million crutch for the ailing British economy.

18th Elia Kazan's film of Tennessee Williams's *Baby Doll* opens to criticism from the Roman Catholic Church over its carnality. The film stars 25-year-old Carroll Baker in the leading role of a precocious teenager who toys with the emotions of an older man (played by Karl Malden).

1957

January 1957

9th The Post Office introduces 'Detector vans' to catch TV-licence dodgers. ☢

10th Anthony Eden resigned as Prime Minister, due to ill health, on 9 January. Harold Macmillan, 62, takes over today. ☭

14th Humphrey Bogart dies from throat cancer, aged 57. Screen tough guy Bogart appeared in over 50 films including *Casablanca, The Big Sleep* and *The African Queen*, for which he won an Oscar.

16th The Royal Ballet comes into existence. Originally set-up in 1931 by Lilian Bayliss and the Irish ballerina Ninette de Valois, as the Vic-Wells Ballet, the institution became the Sadler's Wells Ballet in

Anthony Eden, before his resignation

1940. Having separated from Sadler's Wells, the new company now becomes Royal.

23rd A daughter, Caroline, is born to Princess Grace and Prince Rainier of Monaco. She is their first child.

Princess Caroline of Monaco as an adult

28th Prince Charles starts prep school.

Humphrey Bogart, one of Hollywood's greatest stars

1957 Books:

On The Road by Jack Kerouac
Room At The Top by John Browne
Justine by Lawrence Durrell

February 1957

4th Smith Corona market the world's first portable electric typewriter in the US.

5th Fianna Fáil win the Irish General Election.

8th New film *The Girl Can't Help It,* starring Jayne Mansfield and Edmond O'Brien, opens in New York.

Making electric typewriters

13th Sir William Walton's *Concerto for Cello* receives its British premiere in London.

22nd The giant *Vulcan* bomber goes into operational service with the RAF.

23rd Two months ago, Cuban President Batistá claimed that rebel revolutionary leader Fidel Castro had been killed. It is now revealed that Castro is still alive and that he continues to control his guerrilla forces' well-planned and cleverly executed attacks from a secret base somewhere in the jungle.

Fidel Castro with guerrilla supporters

25th **Buddy Holly records** the single 'That'll Be the Day' in New Mexico.

1957 sees the beginning of business sponsorship in horse racing – the first sponsored race is the Whitbread Gold Cup.

March 1957

A transistorised radio that fits into a pocket is marketed by Sony.

Elvis buys a new home, the Memphis mansion *Graceland*, for himself, his parents and his paternal grandmother to live in.

1st Harry Belafonte's 'Banana Boat Song' enters the UK charts.

7th English author and painter Wyndham Lewis dies aged 74. His writing includes *The Art of Being Ruled*.

Actor and singer Harry Belafonte

16th The Romanian abstract sculptor Constantin Brancusi, whose works include *Bird in Space*, dies aged 81.

22nd San Francisco experiences the strongest tremors since the great quake of 1906.

25th The Common Market has finally arrived: the Treaty of Rome is signed by France, West Germany, Italy, Belgium, Holland and Luxembourg forming a new economic alliance abolishing tariffs and proposing free movement of goods, money and people between the six countries.

27th Michael Anderson's *Around the World in 80 Days* wins five Oscars, including that for Best Film, in Hollywood.

The signing of the Treaty of Rome

April 1957

The first computer language, FORTRAN, goes on sale.

11th John Osborne's *The Entertainer*, starring Laurence Olivier, opens at the Royal Court Theatre in London.

12th The skiffle craze gathers momentum as Lonnie Donegan hits UK number 1 with 'Cumberland Gap'.

14th King Hussein of Jordan foils a coup led by his long-time friend and army chief General Abu Nuwar.

King Hussein campaigns for tolerance in the Middle East

19th Footballer **John Charles** signs for Juventus from Leeds United, for a record fee of £70,000.

20th **The USSR** receives protests from Japan over nuclear testing.

24th **The first edition of the new BBC series** *The Sky at Night* is televised. The new programme, which brings the stars, the planets and their movements into the nation's homes, is hosted by an amateur astronomer, Patrick Moore.

The epic war film *The Bridge on the River Kwai* premieres in 1957.

May 1957

The UK government announces plans to resurrect the idea of a Channel Tunnel.

Proposed construction method for the Channel Tunnel

2nd Senator Joseph McCarthy dies at the age of 49. The Senator first took centre stage in the US seven years ago, when he launched a far-reaching and controversial hunt for Communist infiltration in US government and military affairs.

Senator Joseph McCarthy, seen here in 1953

1957 sees the result of a hard-fought competition to design an Opera House for Sydney, Australia. The winning architect is the Danish-born Jorn Utzon.

Edith Piaf and Jacques Pills at Orly Airport

5th Edith Piaf divorces Jacques Pills. The tiny French singer is known for her sad, nostalgic songs, in particular 'Non, Je ne regrette rien'.

6th Playwright Eugene O'Neill is awarded a Pullitzer Prize for *A Long Day's Journey Into Night*.

15th The UK tests its first H-bomb at Christmas Island in the Pacific.

19th The US announces that its first space satellite will be delayed for another year.

27th Buddy Holly and the Crickets release their single 'That'll be the Day' on Brunswick records.

June 1957

Times Newspapers is the first proud owner of a Xerox Copy Machine. This new device can copy more or less any black and white image in seconds and will revolutionise the office. The machines cost a princely £1,250 each.

1st After nearly a year of testing, ERNIE picks its first Premium Bond winner.

13th Race issues are top of the agenda at a crucial meeting between Martin Luther King and US Vice-President Richard Nixon.

Dr Martin Luther King, peaceful human rights campaigner

July 1957

Singer Frankie Lymon, aged 14, quits his band, the Teenagers.

6th Althea Gibson becomes the first black Wimbledon champion as she takes the Ladies' singles title.

20th British racing driver Stirling **Moss**, driving a Vanwall, becomes the first Briton since 1923 to win the British Grand Prix. The victory secures the driver the runner's-up spot in the World Motor Racing Championship for the second year running.

23rd A national bus strike grips the UK, prompting outbreaks of violence on the picket lines.

Champion
Althea Gibson
hugs opponent
Darlene Hard

August 1957

A device called the 'Drunkometer', to measure the amount of alcohol someone has consumed, is being tested in the US.

7th US comedian **Oliver Hardy**, partner of Stan Laurel, dies aged 65 after a stroke. Married four times, the 20-stone Hardy made 200 pictures in a 30-year partnership with Laurel. The duo were renowned for their slapstick comedy routines.

12th Buddy Holly and the Crickets enter the US charts with 'That'll Be the Day'.

26th The Soviets successfully test-fire a nuclear-tipped intercontinental ballistic missile.

Comedy duo Laurel and Hardy

September 1957

The Everly Brothers' 'Bye Bye Love' rides high in the US and UK charts.

4th The UK's Committee on Homosexual Offences and Prostitution, chaired by Sir John Wolfenden, ends a three-year investigation with the recommendation to decriminalise homosexual acts between consenting adult men in private.

23rd A UK outbreak of Asian flu proves fatal for hundreds as sufferers succumb to pneumonia as well.

26th The musical *West Side Story* premieres.

30th Vaughan Williams's *Cantata Epithalamion* receives its first performance at London's Royal Festival Hall.

Vaughan Williams photographed on his 85th birthday, October of 1952

October 1957

4th **The Soviets have launched** the world's first satellite, *Sputnik 1*.

17th **The Windscale nuclear reactor**
has been partially shut down after a
major fire in one of its reactors.
Significant amounts of
radiation were released during
the fire: these have
contaminated an area up to
11.2 km (7 miles) around the
site. Fortunately there are no
reported casualties.

24th French fashion designer
Christian Dior dies aged 52. Dior, who was the
pioneer of the New
Look, opened his Paris
fashion house in 1947.

24th *A King in New
York*, Charlie Chaplin's
savage attack on
McCarthyism, opens in
Paris.

November 1957

Little Richard publicly renounces rock 'n' roll and embraces God, promising only evangelical records in future.

3rd Following on from the success of *Sputnik 1* last month the Soviets launch *Sputnik 2* into orbit, with a dog called Laika as

passenger. Sadly, the dog will not survive the trip; her journey provides invaluable information on how weightlessness affects living creatures.

12th Postcodes are set to take the place of addresses in the UK.

15th An aircraft plummets to the ground over the Isle of Wight, killing all 43 people on board.

Firemen, police and soldiers pull bodies from the wreckage

December 1957

10th French author **Albert Camus** wins the Nobel Prize for Literature. The writer, actor, playwright, journalist and goalkeeper, who was born the son of a farm labourer in Algeria, takes the coveted award for works including *The Outsider*, *The Fall* and *The Plague*.

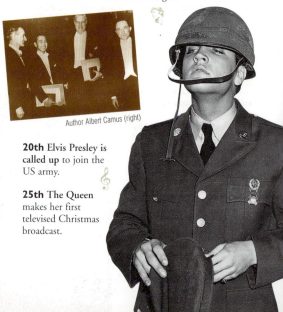

Author Albert Camus (right)

20th Elvis Presley is called up to join the US army.

25th The Queen makes her first televised Christmas broadcast.

1958

January 1958

4th After almost exactly three months in orbit around the Earth, *Sputnik 1* has dropped out of orbit. Despite some worries that the debris might cause damage, the satellite burnt up harmlessly in the atmosphere.

10th 'Great Balls of Fire' by Jerry Lee Lewis reaches number 1 in the US.

13th Sex-change civil servant, formerly called Irene Ferguson, receives a salary increase – in accordance with male workers' higher salaries.

20th A UK expedition led by Vivian Fuchs reaches the South Pole overland.

30th 23-year-old Yves St Laurent launches his first Paris collection. The collection features the trapeze line, a look Laurent – already proclaimed the new Dior in French fashion circles – came up with at his mother's Algerian home.

YSL introduces the high-waist full-length evening gown

February 1958

1st The US puts *Explorer 1*, its first satellite, into orbit around the Earth. ☢

6th Seven members of the Manchester United team, nicknamed 'The Busby Babes', are killed when the plane bringing them home from a successful European semi-final fixture against Red Star Belgrade crashes at Munich Airport. Among the survivors are Bobby Charlton and manager Matt Busby.

Wreckage of the 'Busby Babes' plane

17th The Campaign for Nuclear Disarmament (CND) is formed in the UK.

March 1958

2nd The first complete crossing of Antarctica is made, under the leadership of Vivian Fuchs.

2nd West Indian cricketer Gary Sobers scores a record-breaking 365 runs against Pakistan in Kingston, Jamaica.

18th Debutantes curtsey before the Queen and Prince Philip at Buckingham Palace for the last time. Prince Philip is thought to have wanted to put an end to the coming-out ceremony, where

daughters of the aristocracy and other prominent members of society are presented at court.

25th In Chicago, Sugar Ray Robinson takes the world middleweight boxing title for the fifth time.

Garfield ('Gary') Sobers with his victor's cup

April 1958

Stereo LPs go on sale for the first time, marketed by Audio Fidelity. ☢☢

'Tequila' by US instrumentalists the Champs reaches number 1 in the US.

VERA, the UK's first video recorder, is used by the BBC during a transmission of *Panorama*. ☢☢

7th 3,000 anti-nuclear protesters trek for 50 miles, from London to Aldermaston (the Berkshire base of the Atomic Weapons Research Establishment) over four days. The hike concludes with a mass rally of 12,000 supporters of the newly formed Campaign for Nuclear Disarmament.

7th Family planning in the UK wins a thumbs-up on moral grounds from the Church of England.

28th Yves Klein's exhibition, at the Iris Clert Gallery in Paris, consists of an empty room.

30th After two years on Broadway, *My Fair Lady* opens successfully at the Drury Lane Theatre.

Cast of *My Fair Lady*

The children's programme *Blue Peter* first appears on BBC television.

May 1958

9th A Pakistani official kills the country's premier, Dr Khan Sahib.

16th The 2,000 km/h barrier is broken by a US Lockheed F 104 Starfighter.

19th Bobby Darin releases 'Splish Splash', the first recording made on an eight-track recorder at Atlantic Records.

19th Harold Pinter's menacingly surrealistic play, *The Birthday Party*, has its London premiere. Pinter is renowned for his Samuel Beckett-influenced, black-comedic style. His last play was *The Room*, which also premiered this year.

Dr Khan Sahib who was stabbed at his home

Playwright and director Harold Pinter in 1969

June 1958

The world's first disposable ballpoint pens are marketed in the US. ☘

Pye starts marketing Stereophonic records in the UK. ☘

Alfred Hinds

1st Convicted prisoner Alfred Hinds lives up to his nickname of the 'British Houdini' with his third successful escape. He scaled a 20-foot perimeter wall at Chelmsford Prison to regain his freedom.

16th Motorists keep moving as yellow 'No Waiting' lines appear for the first time on London streets.

July 1958

5th **The Everly Brothers** have their first number 1 in the UK with 'All I have to do is dream'.

5th Australian golfer Peter **Thomson** wins the British Open for the fourth time in five attempts.

10th **Drivers hunt for free roadside parking** as covers come off the first meters in London's Mayfair.

16th **Liverpool playwright** Peter Shaffer's play *Five Finger Exercise* receives its London premiere.

Peter Thomson receives the Open trophy

21st **The UK government** announces a nation-wide polio-vaccination scheme.

26th **The Queen gives Prince Charles**, her son and 10-year-old heir, the title of Prince of Wales.

29th In the US, NASA (the National Aeronautics and Space Administration) is created. This heralds the age of Space exploration.

31st **The Middle East** is in crisis after a bloody military coup overthrows Iraq's monarchy. Young Iraqi officers murder King Feisal, 23, and his high-powered uncle Crown Prince Abdulillah before a frenzied mob kick the Prime Minister to death in Baghdad.

Author and playwright, Peter Shaffer

August 1958

3rd **British racing driver Peter Collins dies** in a crash at the German Grand Prix.

Peter Collins in his Ferrari in Germany

25th **Help is on hand at last for hard-up Britons.** The Midland Bank announces its plans to become the first bank in the country to offer customers a new facility – personal loans. They are due to come into effect from the start of next month.

26th **Composer** Ralph Vaughan Williams dies.

27th **The US nuclear submarine** *Nautilus* travels submerged around the world.

27th **Record buffs** adopt the phrase 'high fidelity' to describe the new stereophonic sound.

28th Runner Herb Elliot breaks the world mile record for the second time in a month. Both times he ran the mile in under 4 minutes.

29th British teenager Cliff Richard releases his first single 'Schoolboy Crush'.

30th Violent clashes between police and 500 Teddy boys in Nottingham lead to 36 arrests.

1958 Books:

Borstal Boy by Brendan Behan
The Leopard by Giuseppi di Lampedusa

September 1958

The new Iraqi government begins land redistribution reform, decreeing that no single landowner is allowed more than 600 acres.

The Central Electricity Generating Board, which has previously built five nuclear power stations in the UK, announces plans for its sixth to be built, at Sizewell.

Calder Hall, the UK's first nuclear power station

2nd A British trawler is seized in the 'Cod War' with Iceland, as fishermen defy a 12-mile fishing limit.

Trawlermen battle against the elements

6th An unhappy Chi Chi, the giant panda, attempts to escape from London Zoo on her first day in captivity. Chi Chi has been brought here in the hopes that the zoo can begin a breeding programme, intended to curb the threat of extinction facing these beautiful animals.

9th Petrol bombs are thrown at police as race riots flare in London's Notting Hill.

22nd American novelist Mary Robert Rinehart dies aged 82. She published her first novel, *The Circular Staircase*, in 1908.

26th Over 1,000 people are dead or injured and hundreds more are missing, presumed dead, as Typhoon Ida hits Japan.

Police in Notting Hill arrest trouble makers

October 1958

The first fully internal pacemaker is fitted by Dr Ake Senning in Sweden.

2nd Medical pioneer Marie Stopes dies.

4th Transatlantic jet-airliner services commence with BOAC Comets.

14th The British boxer, Henry Cooper, defeats Zora Folley in a 10-round heavyweight fight.

Henry Cooper with his three Championship belts

19th Mike Hawthorn, the first British World Motor Racing Champion, dies in a road accident.

21st The House of Lords, the British Parliament's upper chamber, gets another historic shake-up three months after the Life Peerages Act challenged the dominance of hereditary peers. Now it's the turn of the first women peers to take their seats in the House of Lords.

22nd Bubble Cars are launched in the UK. The £350 cars cannot be overturned.

23rd Cardinal Angelo Roncalli becomes Pope John XXIII, at the age of 81.

25th Cliff Richard's 'Move It', the flip side to his debut disc, reaches number 2 in the charts.

The Bubble Car is the new fashion accessory

November 1958

The endoscope is used for the first time in surgery by Dr Basil Hirschowitz of Michigan, US.

10th Donald Campbell has set another world water-speed record of 397.79 km/h (248.62 mph). The new record illustrates well the march of technology – it is over 100 km/h faster than the fastest First World War aircraft!

The Bluebird team congratulate Donald Campbell

12th The UK's Chief Medical Officer warns of the addictive dangers of tranquillisers.

The demand for prescription tranquillisers is growing

December 1958

3rd **The government** wields an axe over British mines, with 36 pits to close and a reduction in open-cast mining.

5th Automatic (or STD) telephones are introduced to the UK, in Bristol.

10th **Boris Pasternak wins the Nobel Prize** for Literature. Pasternak is the son of Russian neo-Impressionist painter Leonid. He originally published his semi-autobiographical romantic tale, *Dr Zhivago*, in Italy; principally because the Soviet authorities would not allow him to publish at home. They now insist he refuse the prize.

BORIS PASTERNAK

Doctor Zhivago

Translated from the Russian by
Max Hayward and Manya Harari

18th **John Betjeman** wins the Duff Cooper prize for his *Collected Poems*.

1959

January 1959

An 11-year-old girl wins a hula-hoop competition in London – she keeps her hoop going for 17 minutes.

Flamboyant film director Cecil B. de Mille dies aged 77. He was also the man who put a small town called Hollywood on the map – he rented a barn there to act as a studio for the first American feature film, *The Squaw Man*, in 1913.

2nd Cuban rebel leader, Fidel Castro, wins his two-year power struggle, after dictator Batistá concedes defeat and flees to the Dominican Republic. A new government is formed amid jubilant scenes in Cuba's streets.

Fidel Castro meets followers, still with one hand on his gun

8th **Russian composer** Dimitri Shostakovitch's musical comedy, *Cheremushki*, opens to the public in Moscow.

12th Henry Cooper defeats Brian London at Earl's Court, to become the British and Empire heavyweight champion.

21st **Frost damage closes** Britain's first stretch of motorway on the outskirts of Preston.

Dimitri Shostakovich composes at his piano

February 1959

The Identikit system is used for the first time to catch criminals: it contains 37 noses, 52 chins, 40 lips, 102 pairs of eyes and numerous hairstyles.

2nd Indian Prime Minister Nehru's only daughter, Indira Gandhi, is elected to lead the ruling Congress Party.

3rd US singers **Buddy Holly** Richie Valens and the Big Bopper die in a plane crash in Iowa. Holly was one of the most popular singers of his generation with hits like 'Peggy Sue' and 'That'll Be The Day'.

9th Shirley Bassey is at UK number 1 with 'As I love You'.

23rd The first meeting of the European Court of Human Rights takes place.

All that remains of the singers' plane

March 1959

18th Egypt bans all films starring Jewish-convert Elizabeth Taylor in protest at her pro-Zionist sympathies.

26th US author **Raymond Chandler**, creator of the hard-boiled detective Philip Marlowe, dies aged 70.

31st Tibet's spiritual leader, the Dalai Lama, flees to India for safety as China fiercely quashes a nationalist uprising against Chinese rule. Troops are under orders to stop him and capture him alive before he reaches the border.

April 1959

The Kew Gardens Hotel becomes the first user of a microwave oven in the UK. ☢

3rd The first test bore holes are drilled for the new Channel Tunnel. ☢

Frank Lloyd Wright's Guggenheim building, New York

9th US architect Frank **Lloyd Wright** – who designed both the only building to survive the 1923 Tokyo earthquake and New York's Guggenheim Museum – dies aged 89. He started out studying engineering but switched to architecture. He also designed furniture and textiles.

11th Bobby Charlton increases his international goal tally as England beats Scotland 1–0 at Wembley.

Billy Wright leads England onto the pitch at Wembley

11th Billy Wright wins a record-breaking 100th international cap leading England to victory against Scotland.

22nd Prima ballerina Margot Fonteyn is jailed. The 39-year-old Covent Garden ballet dancer spends a day in Panama City Gaol as police continue the hunt for her husband. He is the former Panamanian ambassador to London and is suspected of plotting to overthrow the government.

Tights (known in the US, where they were created, as 'pantyhose') go on sale for the first time.

May 1959

🎵 **American composer Henry Mancini** wins a Grammy for his *Peter Gunn* album.

6th A Picasso painting is sold in London for £55,000; a record price for a living artist.

Conductor and composer Henry Mancini

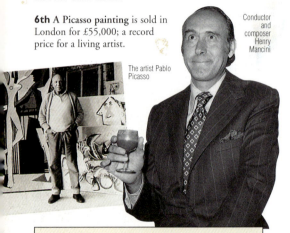

The artist Pablo Picasso

The Motown Record label is founded in the US.

In 1959, racially integrated pre-university education is made illegal in South Africa.

15th The Jodrell Bank radio telescope has successfully transmitted a radio message from the UK to the US using the Moon to reflect the beams. Whilst this is not particularly practical at present, it does demonstrate the practicability of the 'Communications Satellite' concept.

24th A five-year trade deal is struck between the UK and the USSR.

28th The US fires a rocket containing two monkeys into space and returns them safely to Earth.

30th The world's first Hovercraft makes its maiden voyage today. The 3½-ton SR 1 reached a speed of 25 knots whilst floating some 20 cm (8 in) above the surface of the water.

June 1959

6th The St Lawrence seaway is opened.

1959 Films:

Some Like It Hot
Room At The Top

9th The first submarine to be equipped with nuclear missiles was launched today in the US. The Polaris-equipped *George Washington* is also nuclear powered and will be able to stay submerged for months at a time.

17th Liberace wins £8,000 in damages from the *Daily Mirror*, after the paper implied he was homosexual.

Liberace in one of his trademark shimmering suits

18th French actress Brigitte Bardot marries Jacques Charrier.

18th The BBC makes its first transatlantic TV transmission, broadcasting pictures of the Queen.

20th England's legendary wicketkeeper Godfrey Evans retires after winning his 91st cap, against India.

22nd Debenhams bids for the top London shop Harrods; House of Fraser joins the takeover fray a few days later.

Patterson vainly struggles to defeat Johansson

26th Ingemar Johansson causes a sensation by taking the world heavyweight boxing crown from Floyd Patterson.

July 1959

14th The *USS Long Beach* becomes the world's first nuclear-powered surface warship.

17th Jazz singer Billie Holliday dies aged 44 from a heroin overdose. Holliday had one of the most distinctive voices in jazz. She worked with Benny Goodman, Count Basie and Lester Young, as well as appearing in a number of films, before succumbing to drug addiction.

Billie Holliday, also known as 'Lady Day'

18th The **New Zealand rugby union** side defeat the British Lions 18–17.

August 1959

18th The **British Motor Corporation launches** the Mini, a small four-seater capable of 112 km/h (70 mph). The interior is simple, though roomy since the wheels are mounted at the corners of the car and the engine mounted sideways. It will cost around £500.

19th The sculptor **Sir Jacob Epstein**, whose sexually explicit works often caused controversy, dies aged 79.

26th The US tests the Nike-Zeus, a missile which it claims can shoot down other missiles.

Sculptor Sir Jacob Epstein

September 1959

12th The Soviet *Luna 2* becomes the first spacecraft to land on the Moon; it crash-landed between the craters Archemides and Autoycus. The craft took just 35 hours to reach the Moon and sent back valuable data about the atmospheres it traversed.

Russian crowds cheer as *Luna 2* crash-lands on the Moon

26th At Ascot, jockey Manny Mercer is killed after being kicked by his mount Priddy Fair.

28th German-born British humorist and musician, Gerard Hoffnung, dies aged 34.

October 1959

7th The legendary Italian-American opera singer, Mario Lanza (real name Alfredo Cocozza) dies in Rome.

14th The Soviet probe *Lunik 3* sends back the first pictures of the dark side of the Moon.

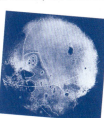

The first close-up images of the Moon

16th Swashbuckling actor **Errol Flynn dies** aged 50. Flynn appeared in adventure classics – like *The Adventures of Robin Hood*, *The Charge of the Light Brigade* and *The Sea Hawk* – and developed a hell-raising off-screen reputation for drinking and womanising.

Womaniser and bon-viveur Errol Flynn

28th South Africa **rejects** the introduction of television.

31st Television is seen for the first time in Africa: in Ibadan, Nigeria.

November 1959

The latest musical film, *The Sound of Music*, is seen by cinema audiences for the first time.

11th The most expensive film ever made, William Wyler's $14.5-million re-make of Fred Niblo's 1925 epic, *Ben Hur*, opens in Hollywood. The film stars Charlton Heston as the galley slave who becomes a champion charioteer at Rome's Circus Maximus.

19th The Queen's head is to feature for the first time on paper money as the £10 note is reintroduced.

20th Europe is divided down the middle as the new seven-nation trade pact EFTA is born. The nations involved are: Austria, Denmark, the UK, Norway, Portugal, Sweden and Switzerland.

December 1959

3rd A burst dam floods the French Riviera town of Frejus, claiming 300 lives.

14th The formerly deported Archbishop Makarios is voted in as the first president of the new Republic of Cyprus.

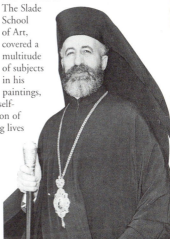

Artist Sir Stanley Spencer in 1958

14th Royal Academician Sir Stanley Spencer dies in his home village of Cookham. Spencer, who studied at The Slade School of Art, covered a multitude of subjects in his paintings, including unflattering self-portraits, the resurrection of Christ, and the working lives of Clyde shipbuilders.

President Makarios

Index

COLLINS GEM
BABIES' names
a ? z

COLLINS GEM
BEER

COLLINS GEM
BIRDS

COLLINS GEM
CALORIE Counter

COLLINS GEM
FACT FILE

COLLINS GEM
FENG SHUI

COLLINS GEM
FLAGS

COLLINS GEM
Healthy EATING

COLLINS GEM
QUOTATIONS

COLLINS GEM
SAS Self-Defence

COLLINS GEM
SAS Survival Guide

COLLINS GEM
SEASHORE

COLLINS GEM
TREES

COLLINS GEM
Understanding DREAMS

COLLINS GEM
WILD flowers

COLLINS GEM
WINE Dictionary